The Gosp[illegible]
and the Johannine Ep[illegible]

STUDY GUIDE

Jerome Kodell, O.S.B.

Little Rock Scripture Study

THE LITURGICAL PRESS
St. John's Abbey
Collegeville, Minnesota 56321

DIOCESE OF LITTLE ROCK
2415 North Tyler Street
P.O. Box 7239, Forest Park Station
LITTLE ROCK, ARKANSAS 72217

Telephone
Area Code 501
664-0340

Office of the Bishop

Dear Friend,

We Catholics have always believed that the Lord is present in his Word, in his sacrament, and through baptism and confirmation in each one of us. In post-Vatican II times, the emphasis upon Jesus in his Word among us has grown and deepened. In many parts of our country, Scripture study programs have become effective instruments for the deepening of our spiritual life.

Some years ago I encouraged our people to embrace God's holy Word. I used the words of Our Lord to St. Augustine, "Take and read." I asked that the Scriptures be prayerfully read. The Little Rock Scripture Study Program provided the way. Out of this program has come an enrichment of our spiritual life and a deeper and closer relationship to the Lord.

The pages of this study guide lay down the challenge to you, the reader. The Word of God can take root in your soul; the Word of God can change your life. The Word of God can make you a saint.

Your friend,

+ Andrew J. McDonald

✠ Andrew J. McDonald
Bishop of Little Rock

Sacred Scripture

"The Church has always venerated the divine Scriptures just as she venerates the body of the Lord, since from the table of both the word of God and of the body of Christ she unceasingly receives and offers to the faithful the bread of life, especially in the sacred liturgy. She has always regarded the Scriptures together with sacred tradition as the supreme rule of faith, and will ever do so. For, inspired by God and committed once and for all to writing, they impart the word of God Himself without change, and make the voice of the Holy Spirit resound in the words of the prophets and apostles. Therefore, like the Christian religion itself, all the preaching of the Church must be nourished and ruled by sacred Scripture. For in the sacred books, the Father who is in heaven meets His children with great love and speaks with them; and the force and power in the word of God is so great that it remains the support and energy of the Church, the strength of faith for her sons, the food of the soul, the pure and perennial source of spiritual life."

Vatican II, Dogmatic Constitution on Divine Revelation, no. 21.

INTERPRETATION OF SACRED SCRIPTURE

"Since God speaks in sacred Scripture through men in human fashion, the interpreter of sacred Scripture, in order to see clearly what God wanted to communicate to us, should carefully investigate what meaning the sacred writers really intended, and what God wanted to manifest by means of their words.

"Those who search out the intention of the sacred writers must, among other things, have regard for 'literary forms.' For truth is proposed and expressed in a variety of ways, depending on whether a text is history of one kind or another, or whether its form is that of prophecy, poetry, or some other type of speech. The interpreter must investigate what meaning the sacred writer intended to express and actually expressed in particular circumstances as he used contemporary literary forms in accordance with the situation of his own time and culture. For the correct understanding of what the sacred author wanted to assert, due attention must be paid to the customary and characteristic styles of perceiving, speaking, and narrating which prevailed at the

time of the sacred writer, and to the customs men normally followed at that period in their everyday dealings with one another."
Vatican II, Dogmatic Constitution on Divine Revelation, no. 12.

Instructions

MATERIALS FOR THE STUDY

This Study Guide: The Gospel According to John and the Johannine Epistles

Bible: The New American Bible with Revised New Testament or The New Jerusalem Bible is recommended. Paraphrased editions are discouraged as they offer little if any help when facing difficult textual questions. Choose a Bible you feel free to write in or underline.

Commentary: The Collegeville Bible Commentary: New Testament Series, volume 4, *The Gospel According to John and the Johannine Epistles* by Neal M. Flanagan, O.S.M. (The Liturgical Press) is used with this study. The abbreviation for this commentary, CBC-NT volume 4, and the assigned pages are found at the beginning of each lesson.

ADDITIONAL MATERIALS

Bible Dictionary: *The Dictionary of the Bible* by John L. McKenzie (Macmillan) is highly recommended as an additional reference.

Notebook: A notebook may be useful for lecture notes and your personal reflections.

WEEKLY LESSONS

Lesson 1—John 1
Lesson 2—John 2–3
Lesson 3—John 4–5
Lesson 4—John 6
Lesson 5—John 7–8
Lesson 6—John 9–10
Lesson 7—John 11–12
Lesson 8—John 13
Lesson 9—John 14–15
Lesson 10—John 16–17

YOUR DAILY PERSONAL STUDY

The first step is prayer. Open your heart and mind to God. Reading Scripture is an opportunity to listen to God who loves you. Pray that the same Holy Spirit who guided the formation of Scripture will inspire you to correctly understand what you read and empower you to make what you read a part of your life.

The next step is commitment. Daily spiritual food is as necessary as food for the body. This study is divided into daily units. Schedule a regular time and place for your study, as free from distractions as possible. Allow about twenty minutes a day. Make it a daily appointment with God.

As you begin each lesson read the assigned chapters of Scripture found at the beginning of each lesson, the footnotes in your Bible, and then the indicated pages of the commentary. This preparation will give you an overview of the entire lesson and help you to appreciate the context of individual passages.

As you reflect on Scripture, ask yourself these four questions:

1. *What does the Scripture passage say?*
   Read the passage slowly and reflectively. Use your imagination to picture the scene or enter into it.
2. *What does the Scripture passage mean?*
   Read the footnotes and the commentary to help you understand what the sacred writers intended and what God wanted to communicate by means of their words.
3. *What does the Scripture passage mean to me?*
   Meditate on the passage. God's Word is living and powerful. What is God saying to you today? How does the Scripture passage apply to your life today?
4. *What am I going to do about it?*
   Try to discover how God may be challenging you in this passage. An encounter with God contains a challenge to know God's will and follow it more closely in daily life.

THE QUESTIONS ASSIGNED FOR EACH DAY

Read the questions and references for each day. The questions are designed to help you listen to God's Word and to prepare you for the weekly small-group discussion.

Some of the questions can be answered briefly and objectively by referring to the Bible references and the commentary *(What does the passage say?).* Some will lead you to a better understanding of how the Scriptures apply to the Church, sacraments, and society *(What does the passage mean?).* Some questions will invite you to consider how God's Word challenges or supports you in your relationships with God and others *(What does the passage mean to me?).* Finally, the questions will lead you to examine your actions in light of Scripture *(What am I going to do about it?).*

Write your responses in this study guide or in a notebook to help you clarify and organize your thoughts and feelings.

THE WEEKLY SMALL-GROUP MEETING

The weekly small-group sharing is the heart of the Little Rock Scripture Study Program. Participants gather in small groups to share the results of praying, reading and reflecting on Scripture and on the assigned questions. The goal of the discussion is for group members to be strengthened and nourished individually and as a community through sharing how God's Word speaks to them and affects their daily lives. The daily study questions will guide the discussion; it is not necessary to discuss all the questions.

All members share the responsibility of creating an atmosphere of loving support and trust in the group by respecting the opinions and experiences of others, and by affirming and encouraging one another. The simple shared prayer which begins and ends each small group meeting also helps create the open and trusting environment in which group members can share their faith deeply and grow in the study of God's Word.

A distinctive feature of this program is its emphasis on and trust in God's presence working in and through each member. Sharing responses to God's presence in the Word and in others can bring about remarkable growth and transformation.

THE WRAP-UP LECTURE

The lecture is designed to develop and clarify the themes of the lesson. It is not intended to form the basis for the group discussion. For this reason the lecture is always held at the end of the meeting. If several small groups meet at one time, the large group will gather together in a central location to listen to the lecture.

Lectures may be given by a local speaker. They are also available on audio- or video-cassette.

LESSON 1 John 1

CBC-NT volume 4, pages 5–11

Day 1

1. What do you hope to gain from this study?
2. Based on the introduction to the Gospel of John in your Bible, when was this Gospel written?
3. a) Which part of Jesus' life is covered by chapters 2–12?
   b) Which part of Jesus' life is covered by chapters 13–20?

Day 2

4. What is the purpose of the Prologue of the Gospel of John (1:1-18)?
5. a) What does John mean by the use of "Word"? (See Prov 8:22-36; Wis 9:9-12.)
   b) Why is Jesus called the "Word" of God (1:1)? (See Heb 1:1-3; 1 John 1:1-3.)
6. As a child of God (1:12), you are to be a word of God to the world, too. What does God say through your life? (See 2 Cor 5:20; Gal 2:20; Eph 3:17.)

Day 3

7. When have you experienced the truth of 1:5 in your own life?
8. Point out the verses in the prologue which describe
   a) Jesus' unique relationship to the Father.
   b) our share in Jesus' divine sonship.
9. Describe an event in your life that made you aware of the glory of God (1:14).

Day 4

10. a) List the verses in the prologue which refer to John the Baptist.
    b) What do you learn about his role?
11. a) What is your impression of John the Baptist (1:15, 19-34)?
    b) What does John's testimony tell you about Jesus?
12. According to Jewish expectation, describe the Messiah, Elijah, and the Prophet (1:25). (See Deut 18:15-19; Isa 11:1-11; Jer 23:5; Mal 3:23.)

Day 5

13. Why is Jesus called the Lamb of God (1:29)? (See 19:36; Exod 12:46; Acts 8:32-35; Rev 5:6-14.)
14. What is your impression of the first disciples as described by John (1:35-51)?
15. a) How did prejudice almost keep Nathanael from Christ (1:46)? (See 8:48; 9:16-18.)
    b) How can prejudice still interfere with following Christ?

Day 6

16. Why does the evangelist begin the Gospel of John with a story of seven consecutive days?
17. Contrast the beginning of this Gospel to the beginning of the Gospel of Mark.
18. Chapter 1 describes the coming to faith of some of the first Christian disciples. What is your own story of coming to Christ?

LESSON 2 John 2–3

CBC-NT volume 4, pages 12–18

Day 1

1. Recall one idea that surfaced in the discussion or lecture from last week.
2. Why is the wedding at Cana called a sign (2:11)? (See 3:2; 20:30.)
3. What did a superabundance of wine signify in prophetic literature? (See Hos 14:8; Joel 4:18; Amos 9:13-14.)

Day 2

4. a) What does the changing of water into wine signify for John (2:9)? (See Mark 2:22.)
   b) What is the ultimate messianic wine for Christians? (See Mark 14:24.)
5. What is the "hour" Jesus speaks of in 2:4? (See 13:1; 17:1.)
6. What is the significance of saving the "good wine" until the end (2:10)? What could this mean?

Day 3

7. Did the cleansing of the Temple happen at the beginning (2:13-17) or end (Mark 11:15-17) of Jesus' ministry? (See Ps 69:10; Mal 3:1-5.)
8. a) What does Jesus say will replace the Jewish Temple (2:19-21)? (See Rev 21:22.)
   b) When will this happen (2:22)?
9. What do you know of human nature that would make Jesus reluctant to trust himself to those who believed in him at the Passover (2:23-25)? (See Prov 15:11.)

Day 4

10. What is the role of Nicodemus among the Jews? What draws him to Jesus (3:1-2, 10)? (See 4:48; 20:29; Matt 12:38.)

11. a) What does Nicodemus lack that is needed to comprehend Jesus' message (3:3)?
    b) Does he ever get it? (See 7:50-52; 19:38-42.)

12. Do logical arguments have a place in presenting the truth of the Gospel (3:12)?

Day 5

13. When have you experienced the surprising presence of the Spirit in your life (3:8)?

14. a) What does it mean to be "born from above" or "born again" (3:7)?
    b) How does one experience this rebirth?

15. Some Christians say, "Once saved, always saved." Can sin take away the new life in Christ? (See 1 Cor 9:27; Phil 2:12; 3:12-14; 1 John 1:9.)

Day 6

16. To be "lifted up" is purposely ambiguous in the Gospel of John (3:14). What meanings can it have? (See 8:28; 12:32; Num 21:4-9; Zech 12:10.)

17. What is the greatest proof of God's love for you (3:16)? (See 3:34-35; Rom 5:8; 1 John 4:9.)

18. How can John's words in 3:29-30 apply to your life right now?

LESSON 3 John 4–5

CBC-NT volume 4, pages 18–27

Day 1

1. What insight has remained with you from last week's discussion or lecture?
2. On what occasion did Jacob first see the well at Schechem (4:5-6)? (See Gen 29:1-14; 48:21-22.)
3. a) Why is it strange for a Jew to ask a Samaritan woman for water (4:9-10)? (See 2 Kgs 17:24-41; Ezra 4:1-5.)
   b) What do you know of Jesus and his mission to demonstrate that he doesn't harbor the prejudices of his culture? (See 3:16; Acts 10:34-35; Gal 3:28.)

Day 2

4. What is "the gift of God" the woman doesn't recognize (4:10-14)? (See 7:37-39.)
5. a) Find examples of misunderstanding and double meaning in the dialogues of Jesus with the woman (4:7-26) and the disciples (4:27-38).
   b) What does this tell you about a careful reading of the Scriptures?
6. When has doing God's will been like food for you (4:34)? (See Heb 10:5-7.)

Day 3

7. a) Various titles for Jesus are used by the woman and the townspeople (4:9, 19, 29, 42). What do these titles tell you about Jesus and about the people using them?
   b) How do your descriptions of Jesus show a growth in your own faith life?
8. Jesus saw something in the Samaritan woman that the disciples did not. Describe a time when you experienced "blindness" like that of the disciples.
9. What does the royal official (4:46-54) have in common with the Syrophoenician woman in Mark 7:24-30?

Day 4

10. What was the sick man waiting for at Bethesda (5:3-5)?

11. How do the Scriptures show that the man cured at Bethesda doesn't truly recognize Jesus (5:1-16)?

12. a) What religious motives are given for persecuting Jesus, even for killing him (5:18)? (See Exod 20:2-3, 8-9; Deut 6:4.)
    b) Even now religious motives are given for attitudes and activities that may seem unchristian to you. Give an example.

Day 5

13. What qualities does Jesus have as Son of God according to 5:19-23?

14. How can we experience eternal life right now (5:24)? (See 3:14-15; 6:54.)

15. Clearly, Jesus is to be the judge of the world (5:27-30). (See also Matt 25:31-46.) Recall some instances from Scripture that demonstrate his mercy as well as his justice.

Day 6

16. Jesus' description of John the Baptist (5:35) might be the description of any saint. To whom could you apply this today?

17. How can we show that God's Word remains in our hearts (5:38)? (See 15:7; 17:6-11; Gal 5:22-25; Eph 4:1-3.)

18. a) On what basis can Moses be the accuser of Jesus' listeners (5:45-47)? (See Deut 18:15; 31:26.)
    b) Is it still possible to read the Scriptures and not recognize Christ? (See 2 Cor 3:14-16; Heb 4:2.)

LESSON 4 John 6

CBC-NT volume 4, pages 27–33

Day 1

1. What is one lesson you learned about the power of Jesus' words from the last lesson?
2. In 6:1-5 who were the people attracted to Jesus, and what was his attitude toward them? (See Mark 6:34.)
3. What was celebrated at the Jewish feast of the Passover (6:4)? (See Exod 12-14; Ps 106:9-12.)

Day 2

4. Which sacrament is foreshadowed in the story of the multiplication of the loaves (6:1-15)? (See Mark 14:22-24; 1 Cor 11:23-26.) Point out the resemblances.
5. In what ways has your faith been tested recently (6:5-7)? (See 1 Cor 16:13.)
6. The multiplication is the only miracle of Jesus narrated by all four evangelists. Why don't the same stories appear in each of the Gospels?

Day 3

7. Why didn't Jesus let the people make him king (6:15)? (See 18:36-37; Dan 2:44; Rev 11:15.)
8. What do you think the disciples were feeling on the boat (6:17-20)?
9. Describe a time when you needed to hear God say "Do not be afraid." (See Ps 18:4-17; 1 Cor 10:13.)

Day 4

10. How is Jesus presented as superior to Moses (6:32-33)? (See Exod 16:16-30.)

11. How can Jesus be the "bread of life" in other ways besides the Eucharist (6:34-35)? (See Prov 9:1-6; Sir 24:19-22; Matt 11:28.)

12. What is necessary for the bread of life to be nourishing (6:35-36)? (See Mark 4:20.)

Day 5

13. What can give us confidence in our eternal life (6:40, 47, 51, 54, 58)?

14. When in chapter 6 does Jesus begin to speak of himself as sacramental nourishment?

15. What is the meaning of Jesus' words in 6:55? (See Matt 26:26-28; Mark 14:22-24; Luke 22:19-20; 1 Cor 11:23-26.)

Day 6

16. In what ways is the teaching on the Eucharist still a stumbling block for Jesus' followers (6:59-66)?

17. Have any of the major decisions in your life been significantly affected or altered because of your faith in Jesus (6:67-68)? Give an example if possible.

18. What things have convinced you that Jesus is the "Holy One of God" (6:69)?

LESSON 5 John 7–8

CBC-NT volume 4, pages 33–42

Day 1

1. What is one lesson about the Bread of Life that affected your life from the last lesson?
2. What is the feast of Booths (Tabernacles) (7:2)? (See Exod 23:14-15; Num 29:12; Zech 14:16-19.)
3. a) What did Jesus' relatives think of him (7:3-5)? (See Mark 3:21.)
   b) What is the difference between what Jesus' brothers want in 7:3-4 and what Jesus himself teaches in Matt 5:14-16 and 6:1-4?

Day 2

4. a) Why did the people fear to speak openly of Jesus (7:13)? (See 9:22; 12:42-43.)
   b) Why do people have that fear today?
5. When will the time be "fulfilled" for Jesus (7:8)? (See 13:1.)
6. What are the ambiguous meanings of "going up" in 7:8? (See 2:13; 6:62; Matt 20:18.)

Day 3

7. What is the irony in the question: "How does he know scripture without having studied" (7:15)? (See Mark 6:2.)
8. What warning for Christians, particularly those in authority, lurks in 7:18? (See 2 Cor 2:17; Phil 1:15-18.)
9. Describe a time when you learned not to judge by appearance (7:24). (See Rom 14:10.)

Day 4

10. Identify some of the "thirsts" in our world today (7:37).

11. When is the Spirit to be given (7:39)? (See 16:7; Acts 2:33.)

12. a) How was Nicodemus treated because of his speaking up for Jesus (7:45-52)?
    b) What are the risks a public official faces today in speaking his or her conscience? (See Acts 4:19.)

Day 5

13. Who are the real sinners of the story in 8:1-11? Why?

14. a) Why were the scribes and Pharisees interested in the woman (8:3-6)?
    b) What was the interest of Jesus (8:7-11)?

15. What should be our attitude about the sins of other people (8:7, 15-16)? (See Matt 7:1-5; Gal 6:1-2; 2 Thess 3:14-15; 2 Tim 2:25-26.)

Day 6

16. What is the significance of Jesus' use of the statement "I AM" (8:24, 28, 58)? (See Exod 3:13-14; Deut 32:39; Isa 43:10-13.)

17. a) How did Jesus argue that these Jews were not truly Abraham's children (8:39-41)?
    b) Was Jesus talking about all Jews?

18. What are some of the lies of the devil in our world today (8:44)? (See Wis 2:24; 1 John 3:8-10.)

LESSON 6 John 9–10
CBC-NT volume 4, pages 42–50

Day 1

1. How did last week's discussion or lecture help you see Jesus as the "living water" and the "light of the world"?
2. Jesus refutes the common ancient belief that sickness was a sign of sin (9:2-3). How would you explain the connection between sin and sickness or tragedy?
3. How is the story of the man born blind (9:2-7) similar to a catechumen coming to baptism and Christian enlightenment?

Day 2

4. How can you explain the reaction of the Pharisees (9:13-18, 26-34) and the man's parents (9:18-23)? (See 12:42.)
5. What kind of sight leads to the type of faith expressed by the healed man (9:35-38)? How is your "vision" these days?
6. What are the two kinds of blindness in verses 40 and 41? (See Isa 5:21; Rom 1:21-22.)

Day 3

7. What helpful insight does Ezekiel 34:1-16 provide as a background to John 10:1-21?
8. a) What are the qualities you connect with a shepherd and sheep (10:1-5)? (See Ps 23.)
   b) How does Jesus use the image of shepherd to express his own mission (10:10-11, 14-15, 17)?
9. How is Jesus the "gate for the sheep" (10:7)?

Day 4

10. In everyday terms, what does it mean for the followers of Christ to "lay down one's life" (10:15)? (See Rom 5:7-10; 12:1; 2 Tim 4:6.)
11. Who has helped you into the fold (10:16)?
12. Who in your life needs you as a good shepherd? (See Acts 20:28; 1 Pet 5:2-4.)

Day 5

13. What was celebrated on the feast of the Dedication (10:22)? (See 1 Macc 4:36-59; 2 Macc 10:1-8.)
14. Why would a "plain" answer to the Jews' question in 10:24 have been useless? (See 18:37-38; Mark 8:29-33; Luke 7:18-22.)
15. Why should the leaders have already known he was the Messiah (10:25)? (See 5:17-22; 8:24.)

Day 6

16. Why did the Jews want to stone Jesus (10:33)? What was wrong with their reasoning?
17. Which works of the Church might make the best impression on non-believers (10:37-38)?
18. What do you believe would make your parish community a stronger witness for Christ?

LESSON 7 John 11–12

CBC-NT volume 4, pages 50–59

Day 1

1. What was the most important thing you learned about Jesus from last week's discussion or lecture?
2. Why does Jesus delay before going to see Lazarus (11:6, 15, 37)? (See 2:4; 7:6; 11:45.)
3. How is the glory of God displayed in the case of Lazarus (11:4, 40-42)?

Day 2

4. What do you learn about the disciple Thomas by his response in 11:16, and later in 20:25?
5. When has your belief in the resurrection (11:24-27) been most tested? What has increased your belief in resurrection?
6. Point out the irony in Caiphas' words (11:49-50). (See 3:16; Isa 60:12.)

Day 3

7. Why does John keep mentioning the Passover in connection with Jesus' death and resurrection (12:1)? (See 11:55; 13:1; 18:28; 19:14; 1 Cor 5:7.)
8. a) Why was Judas concerned about the anointing (12:4-6)?
   b) What meaning does Jesus see in the anointing (12:7)? (See 19:38-40.)
9. Explain what Jesus meant by his statement, "You always have the poor with you, but you do not always have me" (12:8). (See Mark 10:21; Luke 10:25-37; 16:19-31.)

Day 4

10. Why did the Jewish leaders want to kill Lazarus (12:9-11, 17-19)?

11. The raising of Lazarus provoked many different reactions (11:45-46, 53; 12:10-11). Do you know of something good that has caused both good and bad responses?

12. a) How are Philip and Andrew presented as missionary figures (12:20-22)? (See 1:41-45; Acts 8:26-38.)
    b) How can an individual believer have a part in the missionary work of the Church?

Day 5

13. Describe an event or situation that demonstrates for you the truth of Jesus' words in 12:24.

14. In the Gospel account so far, how has the Father been glorified (12:28)?

15. Make two lists for yourself, one indicating types of darkness and the other signs of light. Which has more power in your life right now (12:35-36)? (See 2 Cor 4:6; Eph 5:8-13; 1 John 1:5.)

Day 6

16. What are some reasons people are afraid to acknowledge Jesus today (12:42-43)?

17. In what ways can you better acknowledge the lordship of Jesus in your life?

18. Does Jesus condemn anyone to hell (12:47-48)? (See 3:17.)

LESSON 8 John 13

CBC-NT volume 4, pages 59–62

Day 1

1. What lesson about Jesus' signs would you like to remember from your study of John 1–12?
2. Why are the remaining chapters of John's Gospel known as the "Book of Glory"? (See 12:33; 13:31-32.)
3. Why is Jesus' "hour" connected with the Jewish feast of Passover (13:1)?

Day 2

4. a) Explain the double meaning of the words "to the end" in 13:1.
   b) How are you committed to show love "to the end" for someone?
5. What are the baptismal overtones in the footwashing episode (13:5-11)?
6. Recall someone who has been a model of service to you. How has that person influenced you?

Day 3

7. In what ways does the Church today fulfill the role of servant as Jesus did (13:12-17)? (See Luke 22:24-27; Phil 2:1-8; 1 Tim 5:9-10.)
8. What does this section (13:4-17) teach you about leadership and authority?
9. Is it easier for you to accept loving service from others or to give loving service (13:8)? Why?

Day 4

10. Can you give an example of how a shared meal forms special bonds of unity?
11. How is Psalm 41 used to describe Judas' action (13:18)?
12. Jesus showed special friendship to Judas, who then betrayed him (13:26-30). How might one be a Judas in the worshipping community? (See 1 Cor 11:17-29.)

Day 5

13. Was Judas considered trustworthy by the other disciples (13:28-29)?
14. What is the significance of John noting, "it was night" (13:30)?
15. a) What do you think made it possible for two of Jesus' closest co-workers and friends, Peter and Judas, to deny him (13:37-38)?
    b) What might motivate a trusted co-worker today to an act of betrayal?

Day 6

16. What is new about the "new commandment" (13:34)? (See 15:12-13; Jer 31:31-34; 1 John 3:23; 4:19.)
17. In your experience, when has love proven itself to be the best witness a Christian can give?
18. Name one good intention you now have but need help to fulfill (13:37)?

LESSON 9 John 14–15
CBC-NT volume 4, pages 62–67

Day 1

1. What insight would you share from last week's discussion or lecture?
2. How is Jesus the way to the Father (14:6)? (See 1:18; Mark 1:2.)
3. Do you think atheists who seek the truth can also be seeking Christ (14:6)? (See 1 Tim 2:3-4.)

Day 2

4. a) Where can you see God today (14:8)? (See 1 Cor 6:15; 12:27–13:13.)
   b) Why is it that we, like Philip, fail to recognize God in our lives (14:8-9)? (See 1:10-11; Acts 9:4-5.)
5. What are some of the "greater" works the person of faith can do (14:12)?
6. a) How are disciples to show their love for Jesus (14:15, 21-24)? (See 1 John 2:3-6.)
   b) What example does Jesus give (14:31)? (See 15:10.)

Day 3

7. a) What is an advocate?
   b) Who is the first Advocate? (See 1 John 2:1.)
   c) Who is the other Advocate (14:16)?
8. How do you discern what the Spirit's message is when there are differences of opinion (14:26)? (See 1 Thess 5:19-21.)
9. a) How does the peace of Jesus differ from peace that the world gives (14:27)? (See Eph 2:14-18; Col 1:20.)
   b) Why is a sign of peace given during the Mass before Communion? (See Matt 5:23-24.)

Day 4

10. In 15:1-8 Jesus identifies the vine, the vinegrower, and the branches of the vine. What are the implications of this metaphor for Christian living? (See Ps 80:15-16; Sir 24:16-17; Isa 5:1-7.)
11. Compare the Word of God to pruning shears (15:2-3). (See Heb 4:12.)
12. In your parish what are the fruits of discipleship that glorify God (15:8)?

Day 5

13. People sometimes think of the Christian life as a joyless observance of rules. What answer to this idea is contained in 15:7-17? What is your experience?
14. Describe someone whose life illustrates the love spoken of in 15:13.
15. How can we show Christ's love to a person we do not like or whose way of life is a scandal to us (15:12-13)?

Day 6

16. Show how Christ is a friend who knows you and your needs personally from something that has happened to you recently (15:9-16).
17. a) Are there any areas in your life where you are in conflict with "the world" (15:18-19)?
    b) Where do you find strength and nourishment to remain faithful to God's call? (See Matt 7:7-11; Acts 7:54-55; Gal 6:2; Eph 4:20-24; Phil 4:6-9.)
18. How does your life testify to who Jesus is (15:27)? What do others discover about Jesus in you?

LESSON 10 John 16–17
CBC-NT volume 4, pages 67–74

Day 1

1. What did you find most meaningful in last week's lecture or discussion?
2. What reasons have you heard Christians give for persecuting other believers (16:2)? (See Acts 26:9-10.)
3. How is the term "world" used differently in 16:8 than it was in 3:16?

Day 2

4. How will the Advocate prove the world wrong about sin, righteousness, and condemnation (16:8-11)?
5. In light of 16:13, what is the role of the Spirit in guiding Christian doctrine?
6. What is the meaning of the appearance of Jesus after a "little while" (16:19)?

Day 3

7. To what does Jesus compare the suffering and joy of childbirth (16:21)? (See Sir 11:25; Isa 66:7-14; 1 Pet 1:6-7.)
8. Why did Jesus speak to people in veiled language (16:25)? (See Matt 13:13.)
9. Do you find it easier to pray to one person of the Trinity rather than another (16:23-26)? Explain.

Day 4

10. What evidence would you give that Jesus' victory over the world is already a reality (16:33)? (See 1 Cor 15:55-56; 1 John 5:4-5.)

11. Chapter 17 is referred to as the "Priestly Prayer" of Jesus. Point out parallels to the Lord's Prayer. (See Matt 6:9-13.)

12. If you were to die today, what part of your life would you consider to have given special glory to the Father (17:4)? (See 2 Tim 4:6-8.)

Day 5

13. a) What two gifts does Jesus give his disciples as a treasure and a protection (17:6, 8, 11-12, 14, 17)?

    b) How have you recently been made aware of the value of these gifts?

14. Why would the world hate the disciples for having received the Word (17:14)? (See Matt 10:26-31; 1 Pet 3:13-17.)

15. What does it mean to be in the world but not of the world (17:14-16)? (See Heb 11:37-40.)

Day 6

16. a) How will the unity of Christians convince the world that God sent Jesus (17:21-23)? (See Eph 4:1-6.)

    b) What can an individual Christian do to promote Christian unity? (See Phil 2:1-5.)

17. What are some of the sufferings experienced because of the disunity of Christians?

18. How is your prayer for others similar to the prayer of Jesus in chapter 17? How is it different?

LESSON 11 John 18–19
CBC-NT volume 4, pages 74–84

Day 1

1. What lesson about prayer do you want to remember from the last lesson?
2. How is Jesus' divine identity and majesty shown in 18:1-9? (See 8:24, 58.)
3. a) What does Jesus mean by "drinking the cup" (18:11)? (See Mark 9:35-40; 14:36.)
   b) What is the meaning of our "drinking the cup" in the Eucharist? (See Matt 26:26-29; 1 Cor 10:14-22; 11:23-27.)

Day 2

4. Why was Jesus first led before Annas instead of before Caiaphas, the high priest (18:13)? (See Acts 4:5-6.)
5. What makes Peter a mixture of courage and fear in the courtyard (18:15-18, 25-27)?
6. How can a close follower of Jesus today prepare himself or herself to avoid the danger of failing Jesus in a crisis? (See Rom 16:17-20.)

Day 3

7. John 18:31-32 speaks of the sort of death Jesus was to suffer. What can you find out about Jewish versus Roman punishment?
8. a) Why doesn't Pilate want to talk about the "truth" (18:37-38)?
   b) Are there truths that you would rather not hear? (See 17:19; 1 John 3:19.) Give an example.
9. Barabbas was freed at Christ's expense (18:39-40). Could this be a metaphor for salvation itself? (See 8:34-36; Rom 6:18; 1 Cor 1:18; Eph 2:8.)

Day 4

10. Pilate wanted to release Jesus (19:1-16). What made him finally condemn Jesus?

11. Why does God give people power to do harm to God's followers, even to God's own Son (19:11)? (See Gen 50:20.)

12. a) Identify the verses in chapter 19 that affirm Jesus' kingship.
    b) Why do you think John stressed this image of Jesus in his passion account?

Day 5

13. How is Mary a symbol of the Church as she stands near the cross (19:25-27)? (See Rev 12:1-6.)

14. The story of Mary culminates at the cross. In what situations could her story be a comfort and help?

15. What did Jesus mean by "it is finished" (19:30)? (See Heb 10:3-10.)

Day 6

16. a) Why were the legs of the crucified to be broken (19:31-33)?
    b) Why were Jesus' legs not broken? (See 1:29; Exod 12:46.)

17. Why does John mention the mixture of blood and water (19:34-37)? (See Eph 5:23-32.)

18. What risks did Joseph of Arimathea and Nicodemus face in taking care of Jesus' burial (19:38-42)? (See 3:1; 7:50; Mark 15:42-46.)

LESSON 12 John 20–21

CBC-NT volume 4, pages 84–97

Day 1

1. Are there any new insights you gained about Jesus' passion from last week's lesson?
2. a) How might Mary Magdala have felt when she found the tomb empty (20:1-2)?
   b) Have you ever felt the absence of Jesus in your life? What did you do about that feeling?
3. a) Why didn't Mary recognize Jesus, her close friend (20:14)? (See Mark 16:1-11; Luke 24:13-35.)
   b) What does it take to be able to see Jesus, even today?

Day 2

4. How do you communicate to people what Jesus has said and done for you (20:18)?
5. a) What is Jesus' gift to the disciples in the midst of their fear (20:19-21)?
   b) When have you experienced the same gift from Jesus?
6. What place does the sacrament of reconciliation have in your life (20:22-23)?

Day 3

7. St. Gregory said that the Apostle Thomas did us all a big favor (20:24-29). What do you think he meant?
8. a) What is the most difficult stumbling block to your faith?
   b) How do you assure that your faith remains firm and grows (20:29-31)?
9. How is the study of the Fourth Gospel accomplishing its purpose in your life (20:30-31)?

Day 4

10. a) Who are the members of the group who go fishing with Peter (21:1-3)?
    b) What else do we know about any of them from the Gospel of John? (See 1:43-51; 11:16; 14:5.)

11. How was the "beloved disciple" able to recognize Jesus (21:7)? (See 20:4-8.)

12. What is the symbolism of the 153 fish (21:11)?

Day 5

13. Why do you suppose Jesus chose to reveal himself so often in sharing a meal (21:10-14)? (See 6:5-14; 13:12-20; Matt 9:9-13; 26:26-30; Luke 7:36-38; 24:13-32.)

14. Though Peter had failed, Jesus once again commissioned him (21:15-19).
    a) What is the purpose of Peter's threefold confession of love?
    b) What opportunities have you been given lately to profess your love for Jesus?

15. a) How did Peter die (21:18)?
    b) Why did his death "glorify God" (21:19)? (See 12:27-28.)

Day 6

16. When has comparing yourself to another distracted you from your own unique call (21:20-22)? (See Isa 43:1-7.)

17. If you were to write a book about how Jesus has acted in your life (21:25), what would you entitle it?

LESSON 13 1 John 1:1–3:10

CBC-NT volume 4, pages 98–105

Day 1

1. What is the one message of John's Gospel that has most influenced your life?
2. How does "the beginning" of 1 John 1:1 differ from its use in John 1:1?
3. What are possible meanings of "word of life" in 1 John 1:1? (See John 1:1; 6:63; Heb 4:12.)

Day 2

4. Proclamation leads to shared life (1:3). In what ways has your experience of community been deepened as a result of hearing the Gospel preached?
5. What is "Christian fellowship" (1:3, 7)? (See Acts 2:42; 2 Cor 13:13; Gal 2:9; Phlm 4–5.)
6. Name some specific ways Christians can be a light in the darkness of the world (1:6-7)? (See 2:9-11; Matt 5:16; Eph 5:8-14.)

Day 3

7. a) What is needed for the forgiveness of sins (1:9)? (See Acts 2:38.)
   b) Is the sacrament of reconciliation necessary for the forgiveness of sins? (See John 20:21-23.)
8. Jesus died for the sins of all, even those who refuse to accept him (2:2). What does this teach you about God's love?
9. Comment on the following statements in light of 2:3-6:
   a) "Christianity is a religion of love, not of laws."
   b) "If I act out of love, I have no need to follow commandments, especially Church rules."

Day 4

10. What are some of the ways we "walk in darkness" (2:11)? (See 3:10-15; 4:20.)

11. a) How are John's words in 2:16 verified today?
    b) What can you do about it? (See Jas 4:4; 1 Pet 4:1-4.)

12. What does it mean to live in the "last hour" (2:18)? (See Acts 2:15-17; 1 Tim 4:1.)

Day 5

13. What does "antichrist" mean (2:22)? (See 2 John 7.)

14. a) What is the "anointing" that brings knowledge (2:20, 27)?
    b) Do you have this anointing?

15. Given what John says in 2:27, what is the role of teaching and study for a Christian?

Day 6

16. a) Can only Christians be called the "children of God" (3:1-2)? (See John 1:12; Rom 8:14-17; Gal 3:26.)
    b) As God's children, do we possess eternal life already (3:1-2)? (See John 5:24-25; 6:40; Rom 8:11.)

17. What does it mean to be like God (3:2)? (See Gen 3:5; Phil 3:21.)

18. a) Can a true Christian sin (3:6-9)? (See 1:8-10; Matt 9:11-13.)
    b) How does sin cause blindness (3:6)? (See John 9:39-41.)

LESSON 14 1 John 3:11–5:21
CBC-NT volume 4, pages 105–112

Day 1

1. What subtle shifts did you detect as you moved from studying the Gospel of John to the First Epistle of John?
2. a) Why did Cain hate Abel (3:12)? (See Gen 4:1-11; Matt 5:38-48.)
   b) How do you keep this principle from governing your behavior and attitudes?
3. What is the sign that we have really accepted salvation in Christ (3:14, 23)?

Day 2

4. How does social justice flow from love (3:16-18)? (See Matt 25:31-46; Jas 1:22, 27; 2:14-17.)
5. a) How do we know whether we are doing God's will or simply our own (3:19-22)? (See Prov 16:25.)
   b) How does one form a "right conscience"? (See 1 Tim 1:5, 19; Heb 9:13-14.)
6. A double commandment is given in 3:23. Is it possible to separate the two parts, observing only half? (See Mark 12:28-31.)

Day 3

7. Based on 4:2-3, how would a false spirit manifest itself in Christianity today? (See 2 John 7.)
8. a) What is our best response to God's love (4:7-12)?
   b) Give an example of Christian love that brought healing, comfort, or justice to a situation.
9. What evidence do we have of God's dwelling within us (4:12-16)?

Day 4

10. How can the fear of the Lord (4:18) be a good thing? When is it destructive? (See Ps 19:10; Prov 14:27.)

11. As a result of your study and reading of the Bible, what does it mean to speak of "perfect love" (4:18)?

12. a) How or through whom did you first experience God's love (4:19)?
    b) How has that experience affected the way you love others?

Day 5

13. a) What does it mean to be "begotten of God" (5:1, 4)? (See 3:1; John 1:12-13; 3:3-8.)
    b) How does being "begotten of God" enable you to "conquer the world" (5:4)? (See John 16:33; Heb 11:1, 32-33.)

14. a) What does it mean to speak of Jesus coming "by water and blood" (5:6)? (See John 1:31-34; 19:34.)
    b) How are the Spirit, water, and blood three united witnesses in the Church (5:8)?

15. For you personally, has John succeeded in his purpose for writing the letter (5:13)? (See John 20:31.)

Day 6

16. What is the key to confident prayer (5:14)? (See Matt 7:7-11; Luke 11:9-13.)

17. What is the difference between "deadly" and "not deadly" sin (5:16-17)? (See John 15:22-24.)

18. On the basis of what has been said in this letter, what kind of idols is John warning against in 5:21? (See 4:1-3.)

LESSON 15 2 John, 3 John
CBC-NT volume 4, pages 113–117

Day 1

1. What is one insight you gained about love or belief from last week's discussion or lecture?
2. Who are the Presbyter and the Lady (2 John 1)?
3. What does the author mean by "walking in the truth" (2 John 4)? (See John 8:31-32; 11:9-10; 17:17; Rom 13:13; 1 John 1:6-7.)

Day 2

4. What can you do to be a better example of the love spoken of in 2 John 6? (See John 14:21, 23; 1 Cor 13:1-13.)
5. How does the fact that Jesus is fully human affect your prayer (2 John 7)? (See Heb 4:15-16.)
6. a) What is the difference between being too "progressive" (2 John 9) and finding legitimate new ways of teaching the truth?
   b) Who is the judge of this?

Day 3

7. a) How will the Presbyter's joy be full in 2 John 12? (See 1 John 1:4.)
   b) When has Christian fellowship built up your faith? (See Ps 133; 1 Pet 3:8; 1 John 1:3.)
8. What kinds of bonds would you like to see between parishes to benefit the body of Christ (2 John 13)?
9. Who are Gaius (3 John 1), Diotrephes (3 John 9), and Demetrius (3 John 12)?

Day 4

10. For what type of people does John encourage support (3 John 6–8)?
11. In what ways is the hospitality mentioned in 3 John 5–6 still practiced today?
12. What is your share in the work of truth (3 John 8)?

Day 5

13. What was the Presbyter's trouble with Diotrephes (3 John 9-10)?
14. a) What good reasons might Diotrephes have had for his action?
    b) What unworthy reasons might he have had?
15. a) How would the Presbyter's testimonial help Demetrius (3 John 12)?
    b) Do bishops today have the right to control the access of preachers and teachers to their dioceses?

Day 6

16. What did the Letters of John add to your understanding of the early Church?
17. Select three passages from the writings of John that are most meaningful to you.
18. What overall message about Jesus or the Christian life do you want to remember from your study of these writings?

NOTES